In the Death Zone

Written by Bill O'Brien
Illustrated by Blair Sayer

Characters

Edmund Hillary   **Narrator 1**

Narrator 3   **Tenzing Norgay**

Narrator 2

Narrator 1: There are not many places on Earth as dangerous as the top part of Mt Everest.

Narrator 3: It's a place climbers call "the death zone".

Narrator 2: At this **altitude**, climbers don't feel like eating or drinking.

Narrator 3: They can barely sleep.

Narrator 1: A climbing pace of about three metres a minute is all they can manage. Temperatures are unbelievably cold.

Narrator 3: The wind reaches hurricane force. There's hardly any oxygen.

Narrator 2: It's 1953. Edmund Hillary and Tenzing Norgay are about to become the first people to climb so high. Ed is a climber from New Zealand. He has a reputation for strength and endurance. Tenzing is a **Sherpa** climber from Nepal. He is also highly experienced.

Narrator 3: The members of this British expedition have spent weeks planning and **acclimatising**. They are all too aware that even a small error could result in the loss of life.

Narrator 1: Food, tents, oxygen bottles, and climbing gear have to be carried up the mountain on foot. Eleven of the climbers are foreigners. Local Sherpa climbers are supporting them. Together, they have carried 800 loads of gear up to base camp.

Narrator 2: Ed and Tenzing are part of an expedition led by John Hunt. On the 26th of May, two members of the group attempt to climb to the summit. They are forced to return when their oxygen supplies run low.

Narrator 3: Two days later, it is the turn of Ed and Tenzing to make their bid. They are approaching the final camp, high on the mountain.

Norgay: Look at that narrow ridge we have to climb next, Ed. It falls thousands of feet straight down.

Hillary: Looks dangerous, Tenzing. Almost as bad as the Khumbu icefall we crossed a few days ago.

Norgay: Those blocks of ice were huge, some as big as houses.

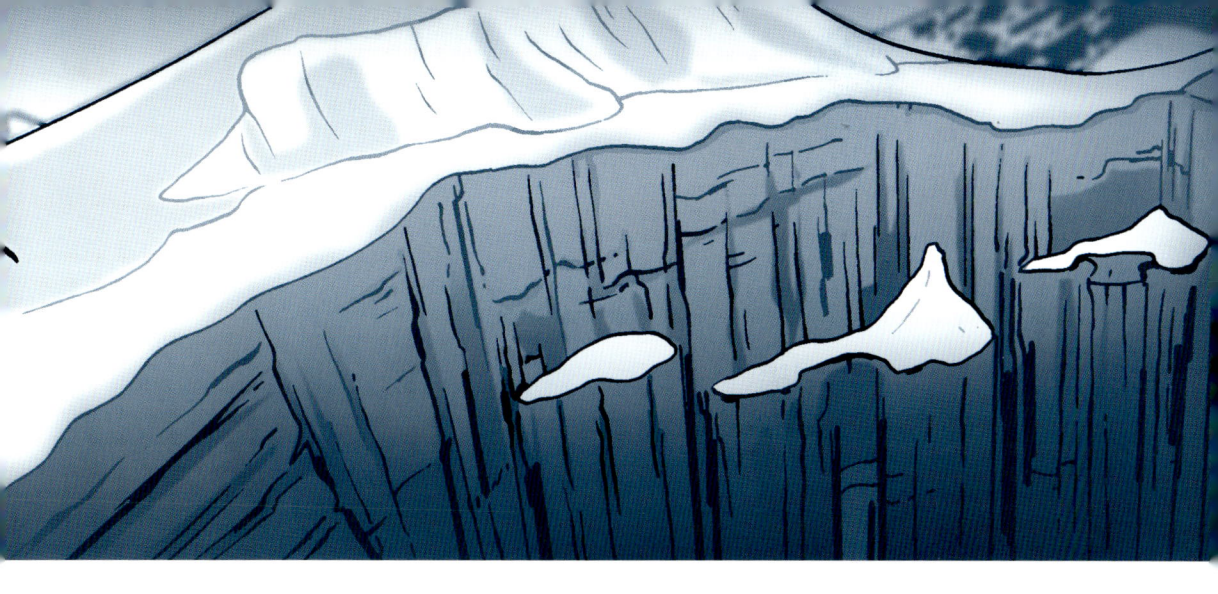

Narrator 3: The ice on the Khumbu icefall is unstable. At any moment, it can fall away without warning.

Narrator 1: To crawl over the deeper **crevasses**, they use narrow aluminium ladders.

Narrator 2: Ed and Tenzing have made it past the Khumbu icefall, but are now walking on unstable ridges with sheer drops on either side.

Hillary: We must be at almost 28,000 feet. My goodness, it's cold.

Norgay: The temperature must be at least minus 27 degrees!

Hillary: And the wind is picking up.

Norgay: If it gets much stronger we're in real trouble.

Narrator 1: Despite their layers of thick, warm clothes, the cold is seeping right into their bones.

Narrator 3:	They stop to cook a meal on a portable stove, to sleep, and to work out how much oxygen they have left.
Norgay:	Here's yours, Ed. I made chicken noodle soup.
Hillary:	I don't feel hungry.
Norgay:	Me neither, but we should force ourselves to eat something.
Narrator 2:	By the next morning the violent winds have eased a little.
Hillary:	What a night! Were you as cold and miserable as I was?
Norgay:	That wind was so violent. It sounded like the roar of a thousand tigers. Hey! Look at your boots – they've frozen.
Hillary:	It's a good thing you slept with your boots on in your sleeping bag. I'll have to thaw mine on the stove.

Narrator 1: But there's not much time. It's already 6:30.

Norgay: Let's hurry. We've got to get going or we won't be able to get back down.

Narrator 3: Now it's really dangerous. Ed and Tenzing are well into the death zone. They have no way to communicate with the other members of the expedition if they get into trouble.

Narrator 1: They're on their own. Each step gets harder and harder. They keep stopping, fighting for every breath.

Hillary (*gasping for breath*):
Are you ready to go on, Tenzing?

Norgay (*also gasping for breath*):
I think so... What about you?

Hillary: No sign of mountain sickness yet. Let's do it.

Norgay: I'm okay too. Let's keep going.

Narrator 1: They are watching for the first signs of mountain sickness. These include headaches and feeling sick.

Narrator 2: At this altitude, climbers grow short of breath and get weaker and weaker. The higher up they go, the worse it gets.

Narrator 3:	Liquid can start forming in their lungs.
Narrator 1:	If this starts happening, it will block the flow of oxygen into their blood.
Narrator 2:	But even worse, there's a third, even more dangerous stage – fluid could start forming in their brains, causing swelling.
Narrator 3:	If this happens, they won't be able to walk or use their hands.
Narrator 1:	They'll get confused and begin to **hallucinate**. They'll start making mistakes.
Narrator 3:	Some climbers take their clothes off, they are so confused. They quickly freeze to death.
Narrator 2:	Or they turn off their oxygen and die.
Narrator 3:	Or they walk off a sheer cliff and fall to their deaths.
Hillary:	I'm still feeling strong. Are you okay, Tenzing?
Norgay:	I'm fine. Let's keep going.
Narrator 1:	At this altitude, every decision is **critical**. But are they making the right ones?
Hillary:	If we start feeling sick, let's stop.

Norgay (*gasping*):

I'm still okay.

Narrator 1: At sea level, gravity **compresses** the air and makes it dense enough for people to breathe.

Narrator 2: With each step they take up the mountain, the air pressure drops. The air is getting thinner and thinner. Soon their lungs won't be able to absorb enough oxygen.

Narrator 3: This is why they spent so much time getting acclimatised at base camp.

Norgay: The snow's getting deeper. It's up to my knees.

Hillary: I don't like those ridges of ice above us. They could break off at any moment.

Norgay: Look out, Ed!

Hillary (*in shock*): That was close. The surface just shattered beneath me.

Norgay: You were lucky to get your ice axe into the snow in time.

Narrator 1: Tenzing winds his rope around Ed's axe to stop him from slipping any further.

Hillary: Hey, Tenzing, it's my turn to cut steps for a bit.

Narrator 3: Looming ahead is a great wall of rock, 15 metres high.

Narrator 1: It's hard enough climbing something like this at sea level, but when you're exhausted and in the death zone, it's incredibly difficult.

Hillary: Look up there. See where the ice has fallen off the rock over the Kangshung Face? I think I can see a narrow opening.

Narrator 2: Helping each other, they make it up to the opening.

Norgay: Can you get into it, Ed? Try using your **crampons**. See if you can wriggle your way up.

Hillary (*shouting*): I've made it up the rock face. Now you. I'm sure we can reach the summit from here.

Narrator 2: Now it's Tenzing's turn to wriggle up through the opening. Then they start cutting steps again, climbing higher and higher.

Norgay: This is it!

Hillary: We can't climb any higher. There's nothing but sky above us!

Norgay: We've made it! I've waited for this day a long, long time.

Hillary: This is it! The top of the world!

Narrator 1: It's 11:30 on the morning of the 29th of May, 1953. Mt Everest is finally conquered!

Hillary: Hold still, Tenzing. I'll get a photo of you on the summit.

Narrator 2: Tenzing holds up his ice axe with the flags of India, Nepal, the United Nations, and Great Britain flying from it.

Hillary: Isn't this amazing? Look at those mountains! You can see all the way across the Tibetan Plateau.

Narrator 3: To prove they really made it to the top, they start taking photographs of the ridges far below them.

Hillary: We'd better start the descent before our oxygen runs out. How long have we been here?

Norgay: About 15 minutes. Let's head down.

Narrator 1: Slowly, they make their way down. As they come into sight, news starts to spread around the world that a British-led expedition has survived the death zone and conquered the highest mountain in the world.